Advanced Mindfulness

The Sky is the Limit... Or is it?

Fifth edition 01.07.2020 By David Holywood

Introduction

Thank you for buying The Mindfulness Advanced Guide! This is a comprehensive and very useful guide to get you even deeper.

Evolution has until now given us 3 well-developed areas of consciousness:

1. Bodies with instincts and senses.
2. Emotions
3. Intellect

These three levels are the framework for the definition of who I am. We define ourselves using our body, our emotions, and a lot of thinking about who we are. We create self-images, opinions, and beliefs. All this is ME! And I will fight to protect my body, my emotions, and my beliefs about who I am. My point is that we define ourselves as different from others and those who are not like me are dangerous to my self-image. Which makes life a war zone!

The next levels of consciousness we must develop are:

4. Heart.
5. Wholeness, creativity and sustainability contribute to mankind.

And there might be more levels such as spiritual consciousness. Not THOUGHTS about spirituality. They belong to the Intellect. It would be something as real as the body, the thoughts, and the emotions.

Evolution is at a U-turn right now. The strategies of separation that have made survival possible for millions of years, do not work anymore. Evolution is going from separateness to wholeness RIGHT NOW no matter whether we want it or not. The deepest parts of our brain are programmed to decide between danger and no danger. This was great millions of years ago on the savanna. If the zebra was not instinctively able to make this decision in a fraction of a second, it was the lion's next Hamburger!

Even though this is not necessary all the time anymore, we elevate this survival mechanism to the emotional level and when we are threatened by our self-righteous emotions, we will fight back as if it were a battle on life or death, just to protect... Our Ego! Which in reality is in no danger!

The U-turn of evolution is necessary. Evolution (The collective consciousness) knows that if we continue dividing the world in good or bad, friend or foe etc., we are not going to make it as a species. We will simply follow other species that didn't make it. Evolution knows that this paradigm must change from separateness to wholeness and the way to do this, is to develop the next logical levels of consciousness, Heart, and Creativity!

Mindfulness and Meditation are tools to develop heart-based feelings, such as understanding, compassion and wholeness. You will learn to accept things and people that you first thought were dangerous to you, for what and who they are. You will learn to stop fighting reality. Stop arguing with the universe. There is no way you can win that battle anyway!

You will learn more about who you are, become more present, and how to distinguish yourself from your mind and from what you think and believe you are.

Content of this book

Legal Notice

The Publisher has strived to be as accurate and complete as possible in the creation of this report, notwithstanding the fact that he does not warrant or represent at any time that the contents within are accurate due to the rapidly changing nature of the Internet.

While all attempts have been made to verify information provided in this publication, the Publisher assumes no responsibility for errors, omissions, or contrary interpretation of the subject matter herein. Any perceived slights of specific persons, peoples, or organizations are unintentional.

In practical advice books, like anything else in life, there are no guarantees of income, or any other results made. Readers are cautioned to rely on their own judgment about their individual circumstances to act accordingly. Think for yourself.

This book is not intended for use as a source of legal, business, accounting, or financial advice. All readers are advised to seek the services of competent professionals in the legal, business, accounting, and finance fields.

If you are on any kind of medication consult your doctor before using the contents of this manual.

In short: Use your common sense and your brain.

Important!!

While these exercises are harmless, I want to draw your attention to this:

When you listen to the Relaxation mp3 or the Shadow Meditation mp3 you MUST be in a place where you can be completely alone!

You can't do anything else while doing these exercises! Nothing at all! You can't use them while driving a car or doing anything else that demands attention, because you might fall asleep!

YOU and ONLY you alone are responsible for the use of these audios.

These exercises demand 100% attention so do nothing else while you are listening to these audios.

The habits of the Mind

1. The Mind is wandering. Maybe you noticed. The mind is always on a journey. The mind travels around in an imaginary world, solving imaginary problems, and experiencing imaginary things. The mind is almost never HERE NOW!

The mind jumps from one thought to another day in and day out. Have you ever tried to examine just one minute of this endless thought stream? Do you know what purpose the mind has? Do you know where the mind is going next? Can you even remember the thoughts that started your day?

The cure is Focus!

2. The mind is categorizing. Choosing good and rejecting bad. From the day we were born, we started building an inner map of the world. A map can be helpful when we are trying to navigate in the world. The big thing is that we mistake the map for reality. When we grow up and this map takes form, it substitutes the real world. And we don't even know that!

Every new input in our mind is validated against what is previously built in. If it fits in somewhere, it amplifies our beliefs. If it does not fit anywhere it is rejected. This doesn't mean it isn't true, it just doesn't fit into my world. But rejection is not really an option. We honestly believe that we can reject the truth, but what we reject – especially about ourselves, becomes part of our dark double, The Shadow, which follows us everywhere we go, and we don't see it because it is always behind us! Categorizing is going on very subtle, on an instinctive level and it is a survival mechanism.

1 million years ago on the savanna, we needed to be able to determine, faster than a split second if danger was around or not. Those who could not do this fast enough became the prey!

The cure is balance and wholeness!

3. The mind is distracted from itself. The mind is usually not aware that it can be aware. The mind is always aware or focused on other things than itself, mostly thought and emotion. The mind is lost in what is in focus. The mind is lost in objects.

The cure is to find out who you really are!

The way we perceive

The Past and the Future

We are programmed! So programmed that we have forgotten who the programmer is. Or more precisely: Who am I?

Our way of perceiving things and events is tricky and very fast. So fast that we don't know how we perceive.

Here is a 'soft' formula for how we perceive:
Data from our 5 senses -> Interpretation -> Reaction

Or more detailled:
Data from our senses -> Associations -> Unmet needs from childhood -> Emotions -> Strategy -> Reaction

This process is so fast that we don't notice what is going on. We believe that we react consciously to events that come through the senses. But we don't!

The very first thing the brain will do is to determine: Is this situation safe for me! And the brain does this by looking in the memory for situations that were similar to the present situation. Those are luckily stored together. The next thing the brain does is to fetch what we did in those situations and what worked.

The next thing is that the solutions we came up with earlier, are always coloured by our unmet needs. A lot of our actions are based on covering our needs somehow and the solution we are going to find in this situation is also coloured by: What am I going to do to secure what I need in this situation?

These needs are always followed by an emotion. This could be the fear of not getting my needs met.

All this processing leads to a strategy: I will do or say such and such... In other words, I will RE-ACT! This means that I will do pretty much the same thing as I have always done! If this is the strategy, we will never be free. If we want more freedom we must look deep into our needs and deeply accept what we feel. This is where Mindfulness is useful. Watch your inner reactions to things that happen, and you will slowly discover why you react as you do. First, when you know your sub motives you can stop RE-Acting and start PRO-ACTING!

From this, we can conclude (a little simplified) that emotions are mostly related to the past and thought is mostly related to the future. So, when you are emotional you are drawn away from NOW back to the past and when you are thinking you are also drawn away from NOW but to the future. There is basically nothing wrong with this!!! The problem is that we lose our awareness in the process. And then our reaction becomes unconscious.

Your Heart is your Guide

Most people tend to believe, that the heart is just the heart and feelings related to the heart cannot be developed.

Nothing is further from the truth and what I am going to tell you right now, ought to be lessons taught to children in school! But let's look at the basics first.

We enter this world with a completely open heart and without the strength to take proper care of it! We depend on our parents and unfortunately, they don't know either. They never learned how to. During childhood, we learn to protect our hearts from disappointments, rejections, and attacks. So, it is very understandable that we build a wall around ourselves to keep people away, so they can't hurt us anymore. Slowly our heart disappears. Slowly and imperceptibly, we lose contact with our hearts, and we don't even notice. We forget. And we also forget that we forget.

This is the normal unconscious evolutionary way to grow up. But there is a more conscious way and even if we are grown up, it is not too late to learn.

We are born as whole and open creatures and during childhood, we divide ourselves into two parts. We find strategies and behaviours which give us what we need, and we also find and try strategies and behaviours that do not work. The behaviour that works becomes so much a part of us, that we call it 'Me' and the behaviour that does not work, is rejected. But that behaviour is in fact already part of me, so in reality, I can't reject it. Instead, it goes unconscious, and we forget about it. We lose some skills here. We get divided into two: The Ego and The Shadow. And of course, we live in The Ego – ME! Not The Shadow. We become half beings!

Unfortunately, the heart also gets divided and this hurts, but we hide the pain in The Shadow, together with the grief and the anger. These forgotten emotions will control the rest of our lives unless we dig them out and look at them. The heart does not live and cannot be developed in extremes and The Ego and The Shadow are two extremes of what once was complete.

If we want to develop the four basic emotions, compassion, trust, gratitude, and devotion, which lead to kindness and deeper understanding and higher levels of love, we need to find balance. Your heart is the most precious guide in your Mindfulness practice. But you have to find it first!

Your Heart is your guide!

Emotions like anger, grief, jealousy, greed, insecurity, anxiety etc. divide you too. If you are angry the other end of the spectrum which is being joyful is unconscious while anger is conscious and vice versa. Normally you can't have both feelings present at the same time, so every time you divide yourself, you make it hard for your heart. Emotions are not bad. We need them to discover our real needs which are hidden in The Shadow (see the chapter on Shadow Meditation). We need them to heal. We just have to do it right!

Some would say that being joyful is closer related to heart feelings than anger, but it is not. The heart resides in the balance of those opposite feelings and bringing these opposite emotions together, will open your heart and make it stronger! The strength is in the hidden part!

Practicing Mindfulness

Mindfulness is a way of being more present and more aware in life. Being Mindful is a way of paying attention – on purpose! Our awareness is almost always focused on one thing in particular. We focus on one thing at a time and move fast from one thing to another. Mindfulness is an all-inclusive way of paying deliberate attention, not only to the thing in focus but to all other things around it. Including myself.

Normally when we are eating, we are also talking and only a small part of our focus is on the actual eating. Another part of our awareness is focused on the talking.

Being fully aware includes feeling the chair I am sitting in. The fork in my hand. Feeling the temperature in the room. Knowing who is around me. What clothes they are wearing. What is the colour of their eyes? Breathing. The talking. Why are we talking? Sensations in your body. Emotions. What you are eating. How does it taste? Just by watching. Not by commenting.

Expand your awareness from being focused on one or a few subjects to embracing everything that is. Open your heart and your mind.

And if you are advanced you also include Awareness. You don't know where it comes from, but you know it is here. You can't be aware without it! Open your mind in the direction where awareness seems to come from. Just open and watch.

Mindfulness Backbone

In this section, we will expand the Mindfulness practice. Some of the paragraphs are mentioned in the Free Mindfulness Intro Manual, but for the sake of completeness, they are repeated and expanded here.

A clever thing to do before sitting, is 10-20 minutes of physical exercises, like taking a short walk or doing some Chi Gung, Tai Chi, or anything else that suits you. Use your body. It will be much easier to relax.

Then find a way to sit down uninterrupted, either on the floor or a chair whatever suits you best and be sure to sit straight up without bending over.

As if there was a string attached to the top of your head and someone pulled this string to straighten your back.

Take a deep breath or three and try to relax. If your mind is producing thoughts, just let the thoughts come and go. Relax more and more. You can have your eyes open or closed as you like.

1. Calling the teacher from afar.

This is one of the new steps. It has been used for centuries by monks and nuns, so it is old wisdom. They knew that the imagination of the presence of a great teacher was helpful. Decide what is the highest possible expression of divinity or love or kindness you can think of. Is it Jesus, Buddha, Cosmos, your higher self, The collective Intelligence, The Universe, God, a living teacher, Love itself...? Whatever it is that means something to you, ask for his/her/its presence and help. The point is to open your heart and your mind and trust your inner teacher. To reverse the stream of love, so it will begin flowing from what you regard as the highest, through you and out into the world.

2. Arriving in the Now.

Use a few minutes to 'arrive' where you are sitting. Relax and breathe – be aware of your breath. Use your belly rather than your chest. Breathe in through your nose and out through your mouth – at least in the beginning. Listen to the sound and feel the air flowing in and out of your body. Listen to your heart, feel your body, listen to all the sounds around you and if you have your eyes open – look de-focused on all there is to see. Just look and do no inner commenting.

Try for a moment to imagine how it was to be 6 months old and you didn't have any language!

3. Focus.

Use one or more of these exercises and do them as long as you like.

A. Every time you breathe you can count. Breathe in = 1, breathe out = 2, breathe in = 3, breathe out = 4 and so on. Decide if you will count to 10 and start over from 1 or you will count from 1 to 100! Every time you 'wake up' and discover... oooops, I forgot to count, start over from 1.

B. You can find a mantra or a short heart prayer and recite it for some time or you can use the HUM or AUM sound when you breathe out. It has a very relaxing effect on the body sending small vibrations to the neck, shoulders, and head. You can say the words out loud or in your mind.

C. Breathe into your heart and exhale from your heart to somewhere in front of you or in the area around your heart. Or use any breathing exercise or visualization you want that is non-dynamic i.e., normal breathing.

4. Relax and be Mindful.

It is time to try not to do anything at all. Use 5 or 10 minutes just to be aware. Be aware of everything that happens. In the beginning, it can be hard not to follow any thought streams. Don't judge yourself!!! This is not easy, but it will become better as you practice. Just go back to being aware. 'Look' at the thoughts, where do they come from? And then you fall out into thought again...

Try not to engage in self-talk. Well, you can’t, and this is perfectly all right! The moment you discover that you are engaged in thinking or planning or feeling anyway - let it go and go back to: Who is it that just noticed that I was fallen 'a sleep' in thinking and lost awareness? Who is aware now? The moment you 'wake up' and notice that you lost awareness is where you are most awake!

Don't try to stop your thoughts! It is impossible! Accept them and just be aware.

In fact, it doesn't matter what is or is not going on in the mind as long as you are aware. Just let everything be as it is. Be aware.

5. Pass it on.

This seems counterintuitive, but it is a very important step, and it will loosen up your Ego, which will be a good long-term investment. It is a 3-step exercise. The point is to avoid building your ego as a new improved self-development ego. This is inflation and will get you nowhere. Use this step to ensure your grounding and a little humility.

Maybe you had a wonderful sitting with lots of bliss and love, maybe you experienced a highway of thoughts and emotions. It doesn't really matter how your meditation was. The important thing is to pass on anything that might be beneficial to others. A lot of things happen under the radar.

A. Choose one or a few persons you know that you think would benefit from the meditation you are about to end. Breathe in and when you breathe out, send healing or energy to those persons. Do this as many times you like.

B. Next imagine all the people that you have ever been in contact with. This could be from a few hundred to several thousand. You don't have to remember every single one of them. Send some healing to them also when you breathe out.

C. Last imagine all living creatures on the earth or in the universe and send them some healing, energy or love too.

Remember when you are finished and get up from where you were sitting, do it slowly! Don't get up too quickly. If your system has been wide open, it needs a few seconds or maybe 30 to get ready. If you stand up too quickly and your system has been wide open, you can get dizzy or even get flu-like symptoms like sore muscles or nausea. I tried it once (only once in 20 years) and it took me a day to get over it, so I'm always careful! Chances are very small and, in my case, and in the cases I have heard about, were in larger groups where there is a lot more energy present but take care anyway!

Do this meditation the first thing in the morning and the last thing in the evening. Your day will get the best possible start and so will your nights.

Meditate without purpose and no intentions. If you try to meditate some pain away, you got it all wrong. Meditate to include rather than exclude.

If you have some music that can help you relax and does not distract you, use it.

Walking Meditation

Walking Meditation (or Cleaning Meditation, Eating Meditation, Dishwashing Meditation or Toilet Meditation or...) is an easy way to practice the art of Mindfulness. You can walk anywhere you want. In nature or in a shopping centre, but in a quiet place, nature will most likely be the best help for your Meditation. But get ready to be present everywhere and anytime!

Breathe naturally and relax. Don't try to control your breathing. Find a walking speed that is comfortable. You can do this by starting a little faster than you think is good and then slowing down until you think it is too slow. Then speed up to something in the middle that feels OK.

Relax in your eyes while walking. Don't focus on anything. Let everything you see be equal. De-focus.

Feel your heart and let it smile. Allow the smile to spread to your body. Let go of everything you can let go of.

Walk in silence.

Be Mindful in your walking and be aware of every step, just as you are aware of everything else.

"Peace is Every Step". Thich Nhat Hanh.

Shadow Meditation

Shadow meditation is a very powerful method of healing. Basically, it has nothing to do with Mindfulness, but it certainly has a number of huge benefits:

1. It heals you and makes you feel more complete.
2. You gain insight into things that robs your energy and happiness.
3. It reduces your enemies.
4. You will gain greater understanding of what balance really is.
5. Improved relationships.
6. Mindfulness will be easier.
7. Improved quality of life.

I learned this meditation in 1994 and in the beginning, I used it a lot. When things start to get unbalanced, there are two signs that something is going astray:

1. Irritation
2. Fascination

Irritation is the first sign of something going out of balance to the negative side and fascination is the first sign of something going out of balance to the positive side. This is the place we all go wrong! We usually choose to reject the negative and drown ourselves in the positive. The mind says Yes to one thing and no to another. This divides the mind even more! No healing!

Shadow meditation helps us improve our relationships by removing the blur caused by our emotions. When we are emotional our perception of others is coloured, and we don't see them for what they really are.

If there is someone who really annoys you and you do this short meditation a few times during a few days, you can transform your emotion to understanding and healing and sometimes it will feel like magic. But it is not magic. It is a simple skill hidden in the mind and we can all do it when we know how to.

But what if when I'm in love? It is a great feeling, and I don't want to transform that! Well, yes you do! Because if you are in love, you are most likely way out of yourself. You are in fact so much out of balance that you can't live with that other person! Right?

When doing this little exercise you will transform your fascination into insight, healing and a love that is more real! You will remove the rose-coloured aura you have put around the person you are in love with, and you will become more realistic and thus much less disappointed later in the relationship. You will be able to see the person much clearer. Love makes you blind. Shadow Meditation makes you accept everything about yourself (and thereby also your partner) instead of rejecting what you don't want to see but do have to face later!

The Shadow Meditation lasts five to ten minutes and you can repeat it as many times as you like. Don't do this while driving a car or while doing anything else at all! This exercise demands 100% attention so you can't do anything else at the same time! Any emotion 'related' to other people can be used.

Get ready. Sit down in a chair in a place where you are completely alone, close your eyes and imagine the person you are irritated or fascinated by. Imagine him or her sitting in front of you and you can look into the eyes of each other.

1. The Definition part. Let your emotion be present. Feel the fascination or the irritation (or anger or joy or ...) as much as you can. Use your thoughts to call up the emotion. Use a few minutes.

2. Emotion in motion. When you feel the emotion, slowly move the person counterclockwise in a half circle towards you from the left side, until he or she is in the exact same position as you. Use two to five seconds to move.

3. Healing. You have become one. Enjoy the feeling for as long as you like, but at least two minutes. Feel healing. The emotion will be transformed into what it really is. Love. Feel the gratitude.

4. Own the emotion. Move the person from your right side, back to the place in front of you so he or she has moved a full circle. Keep the emotions inside yourself. Use two to five seconds.

5. Separation. You are as you were. You are yourselves again. Imagine a bright warm light shining on both of you. Use a few minutes.
Here are the five steps in a schematic view. The blue circle is you looking at the 'target' of your emotion which is the yellow circle.

The green circle is the oneness of the two of you.

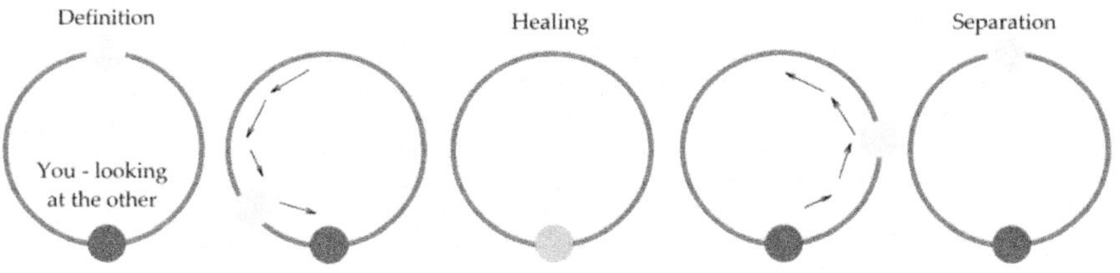

This exercise from step 1 to step 5 can be done as many times in a row as you like. When I use this exercise, it works immediately when I get to the Healing part! One very important aspect of this exercise is that we create our lives and the whole world exactly as we created ourselves. If we are divided, we create and perceive the world as divided. If we are whole beings, we can create a united world.

You can use the audio ShadowMeditation.mp3 to do this exercise or you can do it from this manual without the music and the audio guide.

Download audio guides here:

Shadow Meditation
Relax

Or:
https://www.mindfulnessandmeditation.com/wp-download/ShadowMeditation_us.mp3

https://www.mindfulnessandmeditation.com/wp-download/Relax_us.mp3

Inner Balance exercise

This Balance exercise is to try to hold two opposing tendencies (it can be an emotion) at the same time. This is done simply by when you discover that you are unhappy then remember a situation where you were happy and vice versa. When you're happy just remember that you can also be upset. All 'conflicting' emotions can be used.

It sounds wrong to destroy pleasure by remembering grief and in the short term, it is indeed a bad strategy. But if you in the long term want to increase your inclusiveness and your ability to love the path is to hold your own inner opposites in your mind and your body at the same time.

Relaxation guide

This program includes a Relaxation audio, Relaxation.mp3 which helps you to be present in your body and to relax. You have to lie down and please remember: Never ever do anything else at the same time! Don't drive. Don't talk. Don't walk. Don't do anything else than lie down in a place where you can be completely alone! You might fall asleep!

Hurdles

If you want to share your Mindfulness story you can send it to me, and I will publish it on my blog, or you may go there yourself and post it.

If you want to share how you got through some of your hurdles, there is room for it here.

Here are a few hurdles people have spoken about:

"I'm not good enough."

One of the most common pitfalls in Mindfulness (and in life), is the thought of not being good enough. I'm not good enough at my job. I'm not good enough in my relationship. I'm not good enough at being myself!

Most people are not satisfied by being themselves, so they go on a wild goose chase, trying to find things and events that will make them feel better. Things and experiences that will fill the emptiness inside, that we are so afraid to face. In this case, we really have to wake up and find our true needs at the bottom of the 'fill me' need.

External things will only give temporarily fulfillment and then the chase starts all over again! Mindfulness and Meditation are the tools to go deep into these emotions and needs and over time you will unlock your true needs, which might be something like deeper acceptance of yourself and allowing yourself to be... Yourself!

A lot of people blame themselves for not being good enough. To avoid stopping and recognizing that there is a hole inside, we keep distracting ourselves by blaming. "I have to do better!". "I'm not good enough!". "I'm a stupid jerk!". "I can't do anything right!". Etc. etc. These are just unconscious excuses for not paying attention to Yourself! Stop and listen! Despite what you think, you are totally perfect at this moment! Who would you be if you did not think bad of yourself!

And wishing you were something else or pacing yourself out of this moment, just makes you more unhappy... You are what you are, and it is in fact the most perfect place to apply change! But do it for the right reasons! Be aware and awake.

"My head is so full of thought..."

Yep. You got a brain so you can think and produce big thoughts. This is part of evolution.

You got Mindfulness to help find the place inside that is calm and quiet. You can't stop your thoughts by will or force. But you can use Meditation and Mindfulness to look at your thoughts from a distance. And the place you are looking from is quiet. Even though there are a lot of things going on in the brain.

Take a glass of water, put some dirt in it and shake it so it becomes blended. Then set the glass somewhere and don't do anything for some time. The dirt will slowly sink to the bottom and the water will become clearer!

"I get distracted all the time."

Yep – you need distractions to wake up! That is the whole point. You wake up a little more every time you discover that you were distracted. This will continue for a loooong time, but the undistracted segments of time will get longer and longer. In the beginning, maybe less than a second. Later on, maybe two seconds and after some months maybe ten seconds or even more between distractions. But don't think of this as a goal. Be here. Be in the now.

The End

This concludes The Advanced Mindfulness Guide. So go ahead now. Try it and see if it works for you. If you have any questions or if you think that something in this manual is not clear, then you can contact me here:

Info@MindfulnessAndMeditation.com

Your Audio Guides (right click and save):

Shadow Meditation
Relax

Or:
https://www.mindfulnessandmeditation.com/wp-download/ShadowMeditation_us.mp3

https://www.mindfulnessandmeditation.com/wp-download/Relax_us.mp3

And go to Facebook to get tips and keep yourself informed:
https://www.facebook.com/MindfulnessTraining

Twitter:
https://twitter.com/mindfulwakeup

Web:
www.MindfulnessAndMeditation.com

Good Luck!

Printed in Great Britain
by Amazon

62520965R00020